GHETTO PSALMS

KRISTAL ELIJAH

WESTBOW
PRESS®
A DIVISION OF THOMAS NELSON
& ZONDERVAN

WestBow Press books may be ordered through booksellers or by contacting:

WestBow Press
A Division of Thomas Nelson & Zondervan
1663 Liberty Drive
Bloomington, IN 47403
www.westbowpress.com
844-714-3454

ISBN: 978-1-9736-8864-8 (sc)
ISBN: 978-1-9736-8865-5 (e)

Print information available on the last page.

WestBow Press rev. date: 03/08/2021

Contents

1..1
2..2
3..3
4..4
5..6
6..7
7..8
8..9
9..10
10..11
11..13
12..14
13..15
14..17
15..18
16..19
17..20
18..22
19..23
20..24
21..26
22..27
23..30
24..31
25..33
26..35
27..37

I'm mourning the day of September the 25 2020 your brother took your life because he was envious hateful jealous and greedy you are no longer with me its was a shock on the 2700 block of Elsie Faye Higgins the devil begins his scheme of evil gun shots of pain ranged out as the demented individual seen fleeing the scene in Rayford Mack 1981 Buick Regal. He took a hero of the streets from his people. Shaun Detra Mack faces capital murder charge in fatal shooting of Rayford Mack.

Will I ever get to right the many left turns in my life? My light dims in the darkness under the tree, while the heartless scheme against me. I've had dinner with thieves. They had dreams, but not like these. I wake up with remorse and regret, wondering where time went. It's moving too fast. I can't believe it was fate.

Things and people changed. Some died. I've lost pride and cried in a tent. I was chained and prayed for a visit out of the gate to a fence. My smile was bright, and my soul was dense. Lawless by offense, defense caused this awfulness and loss of common sense. I focused on the things and people who were irrelevant. It started when I was an adolescent, hopeless and unfortunate. Misfortune led me down a path with no dad. I became a statistic, intrigued by embezzlement and the conscience of a convict.

Looking for a settlement, I became a street chemist. My childhood was skipped off the porch to a bottomless pit with swine, unkind in a trench where snakes lie. Everything God sends is a cherished gift. I seemed to forget the devil never quits. I missed my innocence. I lost it all. From a simple kiss, my well ran dry. From the storms, I was drenched. My hands were tied. I could no longer fight with my fists to take it all back. Sometimes I wished upon a star that life could be rehearsed—from fast cars to hearses, verses and voices to make better choices, and blessings and curses. When I leave will anyone notice? God, help me to hold on, stay strong, and serve your purpose.

2

When your feelings are hurt, meditate in your heart, and your spirit will begin a diligent search. Envision the Lord's work. Trust him and believe in his grace and mercy. Only God can foresee your destiny. Praise him and receive his blessings in return. As the waves of stress and anxiety settle in your mind, you will hear God's melodies. Everything that was wrong becomes right. The more you pray, the better you can sleep at night. Through sleep you can regain the sight you've lost. You can focus without a compass. You can finally trust God. You were stuck in a hard place. When you were too weak to stand, God held you up and never gave up on you. Your work is not done. Just the way night falls, the sun will rise. Even though your faith is small, it is still enough. God will save you, and you will triumph.

3

To you, my God, my praise will never end. My love for you is forever because you are my best friend. With you, I have no fear. Life is a blessing. Your mercy and grace never fails. It's only through you that I live to tell your works and wonders. I adore you. I never cease praying. As my knees hit the floor, I never worry. Through your words I find protection against the whispers of temptation. The devil tries to lure my soul, but I go with you, as you are perfect and pure. When I'm emotionally and physically sick, you are my cure. You give me strength and see me through my trials and tribulations. I endure no pain and strive for anything I want or need. I only need to ask once. All my wrongs are made right, and I look forward to eternal life.

4

Thank you, Father, for this day. Thank you for the breath in my body. Thank you for the strength I need to proceed to another day. You make me whole. You make me right. When I was lost in the night, you made sure I made it out of the trenches without losing sight of the bigger picture. When I had doubt, I quoted your scriptures. I figured out that with you on my side, I can make it out of the confusion and bypass the demons who scheme against me and keep me down. I made it out of the mud. I can walk it out and scream and shout, "God is good!"

Through the clouds and smoke, I will make it out of the hood. He tells me that everything green is good.

5

When I'm enraged and full of fury, and when my mind is weary and sorrows are many, it's you I seek. My thoughts were so shallow. What was once warm is now cold and hollow. You found me in the lowest valley and set me on the highest peak. When I begin to weep, too weak to speak, I fall to my knees. Please, Lord. Please don't let the enemies swallow me. In my doubts, bring me up to defeat the snakes that swarm around me. I will rise to your calling. I will send praise and glory to you. The devil is a lie. Keep me in your righteous hand. I have no fear, and I trust in no man. Only you can lead me to the promised land. In this moment, I swear, whether I'm far or near, you are always here for me. I love to call your name. Whether I'm to blame or if I'm filled with shame, because of you I can smile and hold my head high again. Jesus, my Lord, your word is my sword. Your righteousness is my breastplate. I do not fear death. I welcome the day I will rest until I rise to stand by your side.

Kristal Elijah

6

For you were once darkness, but now you are light in the Lord. Live as children of light. For the fruit of the light consists in all goodness, righteousness, and truth.
—Ephesians 5:8–9

When my anger builds, when love is lost, and when I can't feel, I will trust in you. When I'm weary, and my faith hangs by a thread, I will drop to my knees and lower my head. When I lose faith in men, you will raise me up and make me strong again. I'm getting anxious, and the devil is whispering in my ear. I know to ignore him. I believe in you. I know that you're real, and I pray that you will save me. I pray that you will save me and keep me out of the pen. Forgive me for not listening to your voice. Before I committed the crime, you told me I had a choice this time. I swear to you, I have learned my lesson. I'd rather live in the light of the Lord than burn in darkness.

7

Your life is irreplaceable. So, if you made it through yesterday to see today and tomorrow, be grateful. Don't walk around in sorrow or be spiteful. Life is full of lessons. It is a blessing if you are able to learn from them. God is testing you through your trials and tribulations to see if you will fall to your knees and confess your sins. Stop worrying and trust that he will bring sunshine to you when your days are dim. I love him because he loves me more than I love myself. I'm rich in the Lord, and that's the ultimate wealth. He healed me, and now I'm in good health. When I leave an inheritance for my seeds, I will live eternally. As beautiful as the autumn leaves, so, too, is the Lord.

8

No silence is kept. Your work must be shared, Lord. I remember your wonders of old. As I read your word, the truth began to unfold. I meditated on your works and deeds. My faith began to escalate, so I prayed the Lord my soul to take. Once I was awake, I gave him praise. It is only through his mercy and grace that I lived to see another day. Make no mistake, he holds your fate. It's never too late. As long as you have breath, your soul can be saved. Don't number your days; change your ways. Life is not always about getting paid. In your mind, in the free world, or in prison, don't be the devil's slave. Don't get swept up in the waves. Always believe and trust in the Lord.

9

… and that you may love the Lord your God, listen to his voice, and hold fast to him. For the Lord is your life, and he will give you many years in the land he swore to give to your fathers, Abraham, Isaac, and Jacob.

—*Deuteronomy 30:20*

The Lord is life and gives length to my days, although I have stumbled and gone astray. I've been lost, broken, and dismayed. I will worship and praise him always. Swollen eyes from tears can't see in disarray. He grabbed my hand and told me, "Hush, child. This way."

He guided me step by step. His love strengthens me every day. As I pray, I scream and shout, "Glory to God! You anoint me!"

10

Through tears of tragedy, I see God. He is my savior—my refuge. Through it all, he has carried me and protected me from the devil. He is the light in the darkness that forgave my sins. He is my friend who battled for my soul. Through his son, I have everlasting life. If it's peace and joy I need, he gives it to me. When I feel low, he fills me with a rush of love. I pray that his mercy and grace will never end.

11

I'm not perfect, but I'm striving to be perfect. I'm only alive and well because of his mercy. Although I may have stumbled, I stand tall to face and diminish my adversaries. My enemies are piled high beneath my footstool. It's very scary. Your adversaries come with smiles and lies to compromise or jeopardize your rise, but no one is higher than the Almighty. So I humbly fall to my knees and pray to the Lord to live and see another day. I live and breathe to proceed to strive and climb to the highest peak to seek fulfillment within me. I need a shield to block the haters. My eyes look toward the sky—that's where I'll fly.

12

He was with God in the beginning. Through him all things were made; without him nothing was made that has been made.

—John 1:2–3

I am the vine; you are the branches. If you remain in me and I in you, you will bear much fruit; apart from me you can do nothing.

—John 15:5

On my knees, crying, "Lord, save me from my enemies." I'm tired of the devils, demons, and schemes. The laughing and whispers—things aren't what they seem. Everyone wants something from me. Like vultures full of greed, their need for money and worldly things is obscene.

I scream, "God, please intervene!" no glitter n a blitz with Maybelline Wash away my sins so my soul is clean. Help me to not lean on my own understanding. With a sound mind, with all my heart and soul, it's you I'm trusting. I could gain the world, but without your begotten son, I have nothing.

13

Then Jesus said, "Did I not tell you that if you believe, you will see the glory of God?"

—John 11:40

When my eyes are low, and I can't cry anymore, I will look to you. When I'm bitter and confused from being accused, all the pain and strife they put me through, I will look to you, my light, my savior. You are there for me when I am lost, buried in my sin. You found me and carried me to the light. Now I can see that without you there is no me. Without you, there is no life. You saved my soul so I can live eternally. Trapped between these walls, I would have nothing at all, but because of you, my Prince of Peace, the stress and turmoil within me has ceased. Head held high as I rise to my feet, it's only you I seek to keep the devil beneath me. Because of you and only you, my body, mind, and spirit will no longer be caged but set free.

14

Jesus said to her, "I am the resurrection and the life. The one who believes in me will live, even though they die; and whoever lives by believing in me will never die. Do you believe this?"

—John 11:25–26

I had to really go through the storm to embrace and truly appreciate the sunlight. I had plenty of sleepless nights, but he gave me rest and saved my life. Let the jury not judge and rise against me. Let me be set free and not defeated by my enemies. Although they lie and cheat, let my transgressions and sins be forgiven. After I am acquitted, you will put my feet on solid ground. My Lord and savior, please never leave my mind and body. I can do all things through Christ. My soul needs you and needs healing. You are my doctor—treat me. As long as I have you, my problems and fears are diminished. I receive my blessings through you. I was empty inside and lost without a guide. You filled my heart and led me down a straight and narrow path. I feel so completed.

15

It's not a mystery; I have the victory. God has been good to me. I've cried, mourning like I died, but joy comes in the morning. On my knees, questioning, he showed me mercy and made me rise. To my surprise, he anointed me to start my journey instead of placing me on a gurney. I dried my tears, faced my fears, and found a future for which I've been yearning. I started planning. He gave me peace and understanding. As I read his words, his voice became enchanting. Through prayers, my needs, and wants, I felt his love from above. Now I realize what's happening. He brought me to a place where I could see and know his grace. Looking over my shoulder, I kept my head down, but he was my beholder. Now you can see my face full of rage. In a cage, I praised God. I missed the mortuary page. With peace and serenity, I can live long and age. I've walked a long mile. God is good. God is great. He changed my fate. Now all I do is smile.

16

Truly I tell you, if anyone says to this mountain, "Go, throw yourself into the sea," and does not doubt in their heart but believes that what they say will happen, it will be done for them.

—Mark 11:23

Just like the rising and falling of the sun, your will be done. When I'm fed up and want to give up, with nowhere to run, I fall like the night. My spirit is dim. Lord, save me—hear me. I know you are near. With you by my side, I shall have no fear. My vision is blurred. I can't see. My eyes are swollen from tears. Can you wipe them away and give me the strength to make it through another day? Only you can guide the way. I feel so alone. Friends and family have run astray. You whisper, "Jesus loves you. It will be okay."

While I walk through the valley, will you please lead the way? You can move mountains. I want to stay with you. You've guided me, saved me, and blessed me. You've carried me through this dismay. Until my dying day, you are worthy of praise.

17

God is my strength. I will trust him to be my shield and the horn of my salvation. He is my stronghold, my refuge, my savior. He taught me wisdom. He corrected my behavior when the waves of death surrounded me. I was afraid through the night, and he kept me and blessed me to see another day. He is truly worthy to be praised. He saves the weary, the hopeless, and the helpless. With you, I can run against a troop. There's proof in the Bible. Through God, I can leap over a wall. With my God, all my problems are solved. Trust him and give him your all.

18

I must say, my faith is keeping me free. I'm thankful for the ground beneath me. The devil will try to stop me, but I fall before God. I'm only following his lead. As I walk along this path, bless my habitat and pave the way. Try to enslave me with faith. Lord, guide me to the light. In the night, keep me on the outside of the gate, for heaven's sake.

19

When you free me from behind these walls, I will see what I've never known. I will see that you have been with me since I was a child. Now that I'm grown, you will order my steps done. I will trust in you at my table. You will provide bread. By anointing my head, all praises to you. Blessings come down, just like you said. I vow to put aside my foolishness. Be patient with me, Lord. I'm a witness to your love and mercy. Through Jesus Christ, my sins are forgiven. I will be a better servant and pray for my enemies. I will step aside and let you fight my battles. It's you who is with me. No more pain, no more chains. I can't be mad or blame others. I will let go of the past. I wish I could take back some actions and decisions, but I trust in you to order my steps and hold my hand along my path.

20

Jesus answered, "I am the way and the truth and the life. No one comes to the Father except through me."

—*John 14:6*

They ask me who I believe in, if not in men.
The lord cares for my soul.
His grace and mercy and love never ends.
He is my refuge, my provider, and my friend.
He orders my steps and guides me.
Time and time again, you are the alpha and omega—
the beginning and the end.

21

The Lord is my strength. I will trust him to be my shield and the horn of my salvation. He is my stronghold and my refuge—my savior. He taught me wisdom, and he corrected my behavior.

When the waves of death surrounded me, and I was afraid through the night,

he kept me and blessed me to see another day. He is truly worthy of praise! He saves the weary, the hopeless, and the helpless. Through him, I can run against a troop.

There's proof! With my God, all my problems are solved!

You have to believe you will receive trust in him and give it all to him.

22

Do not be anxious about anything, but in every situation, by prayer and petition, with thanksgiving, present your requests to God.

—Philippians 4:6

I can do all this through him who gives me strength.

—Philippians 4:13

In him we have redemption through his blood, the forgiveness of sins, in accordance with the riches of God's grace.

—Ephesians 1:7

And you also were included in Christ when you heard the message of truth, the gospel of your salvation. When you believed, you were marked in him with a seal, the promised Holy Spirit, who is a deposit guaranteeing our inheritance until the redemption of those who are God's possession—to the praise of his glory.

—Ephesians 1:13–14

All of us also lived among them at one time, gratifying the cravings of our flesh and following its desires and thoughts. Like the rest, we were by nature deserving of wrath.

—Ephesians 2:3

But because of His great love for us, God, who is rich in mercy, made us alive with Christ even when we were dead in transgressions—it is by grace you have been saved.

—Ephesians 2:4–5

23

You know my reproach, my shame, and my dishonor; my adversaries are all before you. Reproach has broken my heart, and I am full of heaviness; I looked for someone to take pity, but there was none; and for comforters, but I found none.

—Psalms 69:19–28

Do not hide your face from your servant; answer me quickly, for I am in trouble.

—Psalms 69:17

Save me, oh God! For the waters have come up to my neck. I sink in deep mire, where there is no foothold; I have come into deep waters, and the flood sweeps over me. I am weary with my crying out; my throat is parched. My eyes grow dim with waiting for my God.

—Psalms 69:1–3

God thunders marvelously with His voice; He does great things which we cannot comprehend.

—Job 37:5

Desire not the night, when people are cut off in their place.

—Job 36:20

24

Thus my heart was grieved, and I was vexed in my mind. I was so foolish and ignorant; I was like a beast before You. Nevertheless I am continually with You; You hold me by my right hand. You will guide me with Your counsel, and afterward receive me to glory.

—Psalms 73:21–26

Although you say you do not see Him, yet justice is before Him, and you must wait for Him.

—Job 35:14

But the Lord said to Samuel, "Do not look at his appearance or at his physical stature, because I have refused him. For the Lord does not see as man sees; for man looks at the outward appearance, but the Lord looks at the heart."

—1 Samuel 16:7

Gracious is the Lord, and righteous; Yes, our God is merciful. The Lord preserves the simple; I was brought low, and He saved me. Return to your rest, Oh my soul, For the Lord has dealt bountifully with you. For You have delivered my soul from death, my eyes from tears, and my feet from falling.

—Psalms 116:5–9

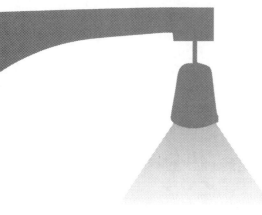

He said, "The Lord is my rock, my fortress and my deliverer; my God is my rock, in whom I take refuge, my shield, and the horn of my salvation. He is my stronghold, my refuge, and my savior—from violent people you save me. "I called to the Lord, who is worthy of praise, and have been saved from my enemies. The waves of death swirled about me; the torrents of destruction overwhelmed me. The cords of the grave coiled around me; the snares of death confronted me. "In my distress I called to the Lord; I called out to my God. From his temple he heard my voice; my cry came to his ears.

—2 Samuel 22:2–7

25

While he himself went a day's journey into the wilderness. He came to a broom bush, sat down under it and prayed that he might die. "I have had enough, Lord," he said. "Take my life; I am no better than my ancestors." Then he lay down under the bush and fell asleep.

All at once an angel touched him and said, "Get up and eat." He looked around, and there by his head was some bread baked over hot coals, and a jar of water. He ate and drank and then lay down again.

The angel of the Lord came back a second time and touched him and said, "Get up and eat, for the journey is too much for you." So he got up and ate and drank. Strengthened by that food, he traveled forty days and forty nights until he reached Horeb, the mountain of God.

—1 Kings 19:4–8

But my God shall supply all your need according to his riches in glory by Christ Jesus.

—Philippians 4:19

Finally, brothers and sisters, whatever is true, whatever is noble, whatever is right, whatever is pure, whatever is lovely, whatever is admirable—if anything is excellent or praiseworthy—think about such things. [9] Whatever you have learned or received or heard from me, or seen in me—put it into practice. And the God of peace will be with you.

—Philippians 4:8–9

26

I have been with you wherever you have gone, and I have cut off all your enemies from before you. Now I will make your name great, like the names of the greatest men on earth.

—2 Samuel 7:9

I was pushed so hard I was falling, but the Lord helped me. The Lord is my strength and my song, and He has become my salvation.

—Psalm 118:13–14

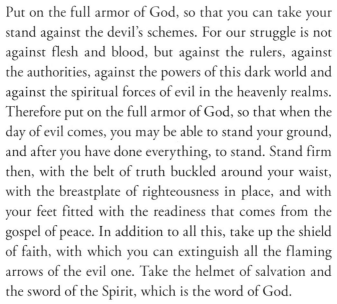

Put on the full armor of God, so that you can take your stand against the devil's schemes. For our struggle is not against flesh and blood, but against the rulers, against the authorities, against the powers of this dark world and against the spiritual forces of evil in the heavenly realms. Therefore put on the full armor of God, so that when the day of evil comes, you may be able to stand your ground, and after you have done everything, to stand. Stand firm then, with the belt of truth buckled around your waist, with the breastplate of righteousness in place, and with your feet fitted with the readiness that comes from the gospel of peace. In addition to all this, take up the shield of faith, with which you can extinguish all the flaming arrows of the evil one. Take the helmet of salvation and the sword of the Spirit, which is the word of God.

And pray in the Spirit on all occasions with all kinds of prayers and requests. With this in mind, be alert and always keep on praying for all the Lord's people. Pray also for me, that whenever I speak, words may be given me so that I will fearlessly make known the mystery of the gospel, for which I am an ambassador in chains. Pray that I may declare it fearlessly, as I should.

—Ephesians 6:11–20

27

The Lord is my light and my salvation—whom shall I fear? The Lord is the stronghold of my life—of whom shall I be afraid?

—Psalm 27:1

A true Shepard of the hood with bad u turned to good you carried so many same day I passed by to see strangely your were gone. Heard the word trouble had came along in the environment we live in constant visits from different spirits seemed to find you But, MAC the special one blessed and favored by so many because of your humbleness you gave and shared with plenty in the slum you made it fun .You gave hope and wisdom you never ran away always Led . I remembered what you said you you chose the life of a prince I thought maybe Your Mother wanted u in a different life style.Moments later u stumbled in the path of a traitor a true hater sadly it was your brother your offerings and good spirits kept people laughing you never said no only "Get Out Che"knowing you were so spiritual and always sharing daily acts of caring you gave me opportunities and showed me favor and for that I wish I could repay you it wasn't until you were gone that I realized why you couldn't leave you had a lot of people depending on you and responsibilities you handled with ease you were a blessing to many families you will truly be missed I know one day with God I will see you again my friend" Ha Man".

In Loving Memory of

Rayford Earl Mack

Sunrise: May 3, 1976   Sunset: September 25, 2020

Viewing
Friday, October 2, 2020
10:00 am - 8:00 pm

James Lomax Memorial Chapel

Lomax Funeral Home

2703 Elsie Faye Heggins St.
Dallas, Texas 75215

Printed in the United States
by Baker & Taylor Publisher Services